Killer Disasters

VOLCANOES

Doreen Gonzales

PowerKiDS press
New York

Published in 2013 by The Rosen Publishing Group, Inc.
29 East 21st Street, New York, NY 10010

First Edition

Editor: Amelie von Zumbusch
Book Design: Greg Tucker
Layout Design: Julio Gil

Photo Credits: Cover wdeon/Shutterstock.com; p. 4 © Steve Terrill/age fotostock; pp. 5 (top) Vulkanette/Shutterstock.com; p. 5 (bottom) Sonny Tumbelaka/AFP/Getty Images; p. 6 Robert Rozbora/Shutterstock.com; p. 7 Joe Carini/Perspectives/Getty Images; p. 8 Chlaus Lotscher/Peter Arnold/Getty Images; p. 9 (top) Tony Northrup/Shutterstock.com; p. 9 (bottom) Philippe Bourseiller/The Image Bank/Getty Images; p. 10 Bloomberg/Getty Images; p. 11 (top) Leif R. Jansson/AFP/Getty Images; p. 11 (bottom) Emmanuel Dunand/AFP/Getty Images; pp. 12–13 Halldor Kolbeins/AFP/Getty Images; p. 14 Hulton Archive/Getty Images; p. 15 Byelikova Oksana/Shutterstock.com; p. 16 STF/AFP/Getty Images; p. 17 Carlos Angel/Getty Images; pp. 18–19 witchcraft/Shutterstock.com; p. 20 © Ragnar Th. Sigurdsson/age fotostock; p. 21 Robert Madden/National Geographic/Getty Images; p. 22 AFP/Getty Images.

Library of Congress Cataloging-in-Publication Data

Gonzales, Doreen.
Volcanoes / by Doreen Gonzales. — 1st ed.
p. cm. — (Killer disasters)
Includes index.
ISBN 978-1-4488-7441-5 (library binding) – ISBN 978-1-4488-7514-6 (pbk.) –
ISBN 978-1-4488-7588-7 (6-pack)
1. Volcanoes—Juvenile literature. I. Title.
QE521.3.G66 2013
551.21—dc23

2011052948

Manufactured in the United States of America

CPSIA Compliance Information: Batch #B3S12PK: For Further Information contact Rosen Publishing, New York, New York at 1-800-237-9932

Contents

A HOLE IN THE EARTH

A volcano is a hole in the ground that reaches far underground. Sometimes rocks and gas from deep underground come out of the hole, or **vent**. This is known as an **eruption**.

In some eruptions, hot, liquid rock called **lava** flows from the vent. Other eruptions shoot lava high into the air. Volcanic eruptions can be fantastic to watch.

Mount St. Helens, in Washington, had a big eruption in 1980. The eruption changed the volcano's shape.

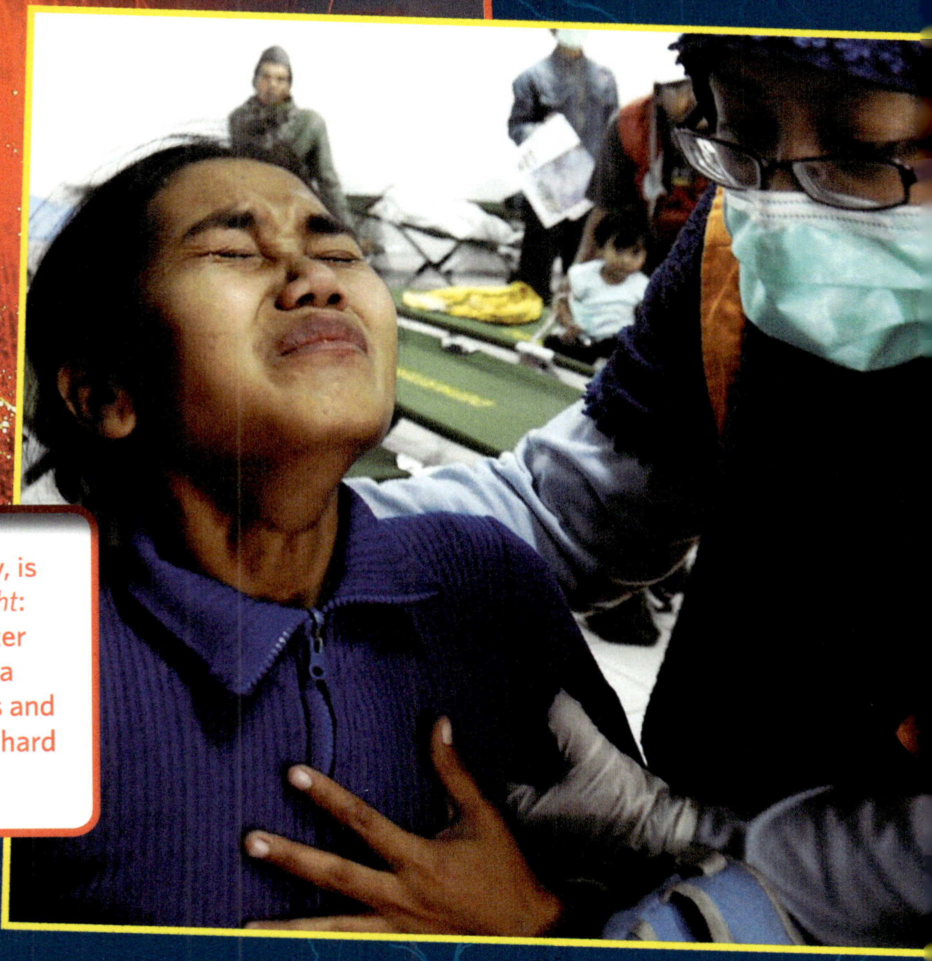

Above: Mount Stromboli, in Italy, is a volcano that erupts often. *Right*: This woman is being treated after an eruption of Gunung Merapi, a volcano in Indonesia. The gases and ash from a volcano can make it hard for people to breathe.

However, they are also dangerous. They can cause a lot of damage. Some eruptions kill people.

Eruptions can cause other deadly disasters, too. For example, eruptions near the ocean or underwater can set off huge waves called **tsunamis**. Tsunamis can cause flooding along coasts.

BURSTING THROUGH

Earth's outside layer is called the **crust**. It is made up of huge plates of rock that fit together like a puzzle. Below the plates are rocks and **magma**. Magma is rock that is so hot that it is liquid.

This long gap in the ground is one of the places in Iceland where you can see the Eurasian and North American plates meeting.

The volcano Mauna Loa, in Hawaii, formed over a hot spot.

Sometimes magma rises up between two plates. If it spills out onto Earth's surface, it causes a volcanic eruption. Erupting magma is known as lava.

Volcanoes also form over **hot spots**. Hot spots are places where especially hot magma pushes its way up through a plate. The magma collects in a pool under the crust and sometimes bursts through.

SHIELDS AND CONES

Different kinds of volcanoes erupt in different ways. Shield volcanoes, for example, are low and wide. They form at hot spots. Lava spills from their holes, or vents. It then cools and hardens to build a gently sloping hill.

Cinder cones are cone-shaped volcanoes made when balls of lava shoot out of a vent. The force of the

Nicaragua's Cerro Negro is a cinder cone.

Above: Arenal Volcano, in Costa Rica, is a composite volcano. Composite volcanoes are also called stratovolcanoes. *Right*: Piton de la Fournaise, on the island of Réunion, is a shield volcano.

explosion breaks the cooling lava into small pieces called cinders. Most cinder cones have **craters**, or bowl-like dents on top.

Composite volcanoes are also shaped like cones. Both lava and rock erupt from them and pile up along their sides.

FAR-OFF EFFECTS

The biggest volcanic eruption in recorded history took place in Indonesia in 1815. Mount Tambora erupted, shooting ash 28 miles (45 km) into the air and killing about 100,000 people.

The eruption created a gas cloud that blocked warmth from the Sun. It made weather around the world much

This is what Mount Tambora looks like today. It is also known as Tamboro.

Above: These people were stranded in an airport outside of Stockholm, Sweden, because of Eyjafjallajökull's 2010 eruption. *Right*: Ash from Eyjafjallajökull darkened the skies above Iceland in 2010.

cooler than usual. This made crops die. Thousands more people then died of **starvation**.

The 2010 eruption of a volcano in Iceland caused a different problem. Eyjafjallajökull erupted for three months, sending ash all the way to Europe. Airplanes could not fly through the ash, so air travel was stopped for days.

Disaster in Iceland!

Date:	**March 20–June 23, 2010**
Volcano's name:	**Eyjafjallajökull**
Volcano type:	**Composite, covered with ice**
Summit elevation:	**5,466 feet (1,666 m)**

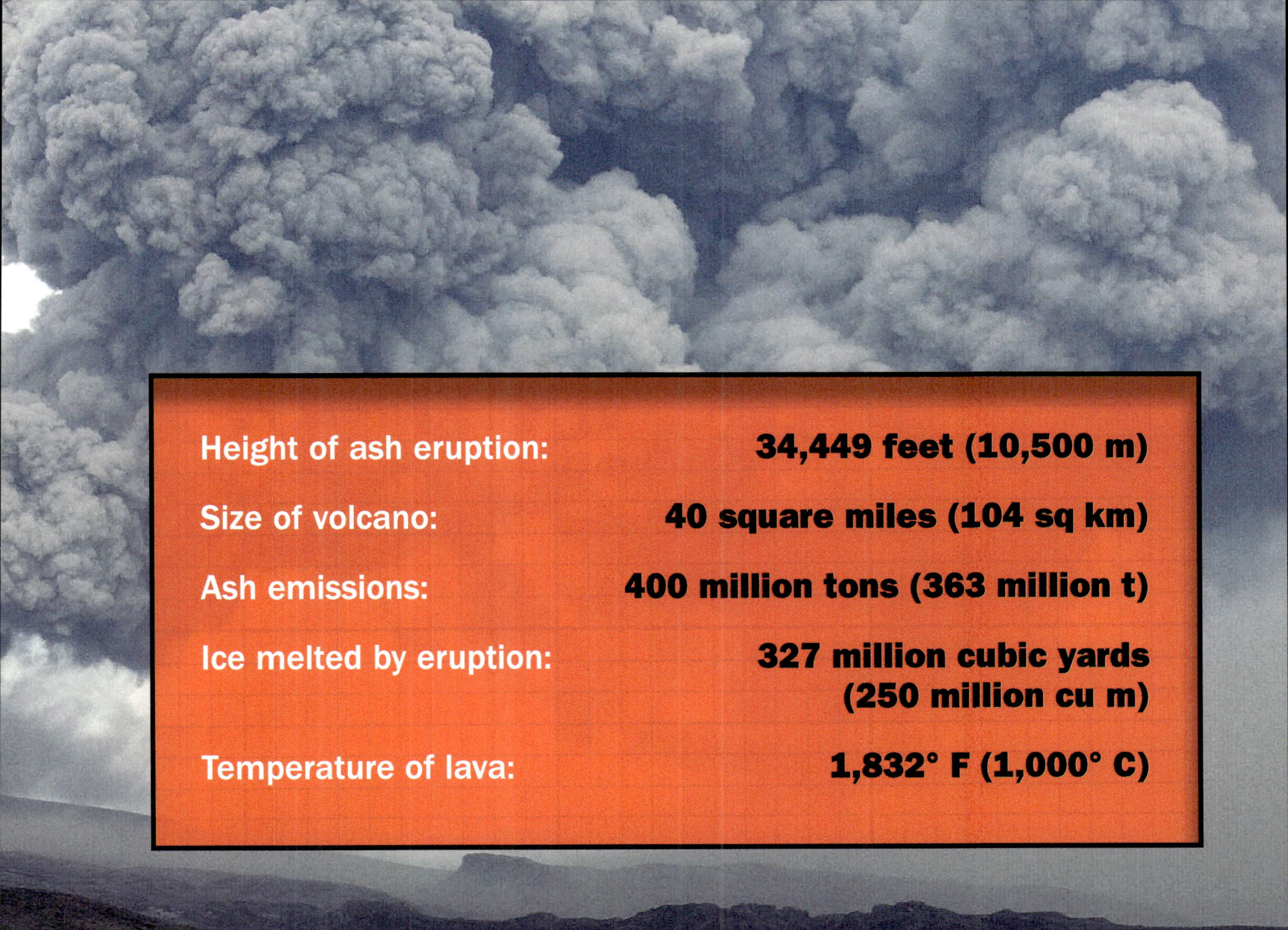

Height of ash eruption:	**34,449 feet (10,500 m)**
Size of volcano:	**40 square miles (104 sq km)**
Ash emissions:	**400 million tons (363 million t)**
Ice melted by eruption:	**327 million cubic yards (250 million cu m)**
Temperature of lava:	**1,832° F (1,000° C)**

KRAKATAU

Most of Earth's volcanoes are in an area around the Pacific Ocean known as the Ring of Fire. Krakatau, a volcano in Indonesia, is one.

Krakatau is best known for its powerful eruption in 1883. That eruption destroyed much of the island on which the volcano sat. The blast it made was heard 3,000 miles (4,800 km) away.

This drawing shows the 1883 eruption of Krakatau. Krakatau is also known as Krakatoa.

In 1927, an island volcano rose from the water in the spot where Krakatau once stood. It was named Anak Krakatau. This means "child of Krakatau."

Krakatau's eruption killed thousands of people on the island. Then, it set off a tsunami that killed thousands more on islands nearby. Scientists think that ash from the eruption blocked enough sunlight to cause cooler temperatures around the world for several years.

DEADLY MUD

Nevado del Ruiz is an ice-covered volcano in Colombia. Heat from its eruptions often melts the ice. The water this produces mixes with the material coming out of the volcano. This makes a heavy mud that slides down the mountain, washing away everything in its path. It is called a **lahar**.

Sadly, the 1985 lahar killed most of the people living in Armero.

You can see the glaciers, or thick sheets of ice, covering Nevado del Ruiz in this picture of the volcano.

In 1985, an eruption of Nevado del Ruiz created a deadly lahar. The mud became deeper and deeper as it moved downhill. Within 3 hours, a wall of mud 130 feet (40 m) tall was sweeping through the town of Armero. The mud buried what it did not carry away. The eruption killed 23,000 people.

FORGOTTEN TOWNS

One of today's most dangerous volcanoes is Mount Vesuvius, in Italy. It could erupt at any time, yet three million people still live near its slopes.

Mount Vesuvius has erupted many times in the past. In AD 79, the volcano shot out so much ash and rock that the nearby towns of Pompeii and Herculaneum were buried. Most of the people living there were killed as they tried to escape.

In time, people forgot about the towns. Then their remains were discovered in the 1700s. As scientists dug through the ruins, they learned much about life long ago.

The ruins of Herculaneum are in the front of this picture. The modern-day town of Ercolano sits behind the ruins. Mount Vesuvius is behind Ercolano.

VOLCANO WATCH

Several US volcanoes have **observatories** near them. These are places where scientists can study volcanoes up close. The scientists there are always watching for movements in the ground that could mean an eruption is coming.

Scientists also study the rocks near volcanoes to learn what is inside Earth. They study the gases coming

These scientists are measuring how much ash fell in a 2011 eruption of Grímsvötn, a volcano in Iceland. They are also taking samples of the ash to study.

out of vents, too. This helps them figure out if an eruption is coming. Working close to volcanoes is dangerous work, so these scientists must be very careful.

Scientists use the information they gather to create **models** of volcanoes on computers and in labs. These help them understand how volcanoes act.

This brave scientist is studying Mauna Ulu. Mauna Ulu is part of the volcano Kilauea, in Hawaii.

BE READY!

Scientists can tell if a volcano is likely to erupt sometime during the next few years. They are not often able to be more exact, though.

If you live near a volcano, keep an emergency kit ready. It should include a mask, flashlight, and battery-operated radio. Stay inside during an eruption and be ready to leave the area if needed. Volcanic eruptions are dangerous, so always be ready to keep yourself safe.

The people living nearby had to evacuate, or leave for safety, when Indonesia's Mount Gamalama started erupting in 2011.

GLOSSARY

CRATERS (KRAY-turz) Large, bowl-shaped dips.

CRUST (KRUST) The outside of a planet.

ERUPTION (ih-RUP-shun) The explosion of gases, smoke, or lava from a volcano.

HOT SPOTS (HOT SPOTS) Places in the middle of plates where molten rock reaches Earth's surface.

LAHAR (LAH-hahr) A mudslide that forms when water mixes with things that come out of a volcano.

LAVA (LAH-vuh) Hot, melted rock that comes out of a volcano.

MAGMA (MAG-muh) Hot, melted rock inside Earth.

MODELS (MAH-dulz) Small copies of things.

OBSERVATORIES (ub-ZUR-vuh-tor-eez) Buildings where scientists study things by watching them.

STARVATION (star-VAY-shun) The act of suffering or dying from hunger.

TSUNAMIS (soo-NAH-meez) Series of waves that are often caused by movements in Earth's crust.

VENT (VENT) An opening.

INDEX

WEBSITES

Due to the changing nature of Internet links, PowerKids Press has developed an online list of websites related to the subject of this book. This site is updated regularly. Please use this link to access the list: www.powerkidslinks.com/kd/volc/